7/12

A to Z of

Friends and Family

Tracy Nelson Maurer

Rourke Publishing LLC
Vero Beach, Florida 32964

About The Author:

Tracy Nelson Maurer specializes in nonfiction and business writing. Her most recently published children's books include the Green Thumb Guides series, also from the Rourke Book Company. A University of Minnesota graduate, Tracy lives with her husband Mike and two children in Superior, Wisconsin.

Acknowledgments:

With appreciation to Margaret and Thomas for their joyful assistance in developing this series, and to Lois M. Nelson for her editing and enthusiastic support.

PHOTO CREDITS:
© Photodisc, Cover; © Linda Dingman, page 13, 24, 32, 26, 46, 48; © Diane Farleo, page 34; © Craig Lopetz, page 20; © Lois M. Nelson, page 6, 8, 10, 12, 14, 18, 22, 26, 28, 30, 40; © Cahill Photography of Amery, WI, page 42.

Library of Congress Cataloging-in-Publication Data

Maurer, Tracy, 1965–
   A to Z of friends and family / Tracy Nelson Maurer.
     p. cm. — (A to Z)
   ISBN 1-58952-060-2
   1. Family—Juvenile literature. 2. Friendship—Juvenile literature. [1. Family. 2. Friendship. 3. Alphabet.] I. Title

HQ744 .M39 2001
306.85—dc21

2001018591

Printed in the USA

Aa

Adoption makes a new family.

Bb

Brothers are good playmates.

A B C D E F G H I J K L M

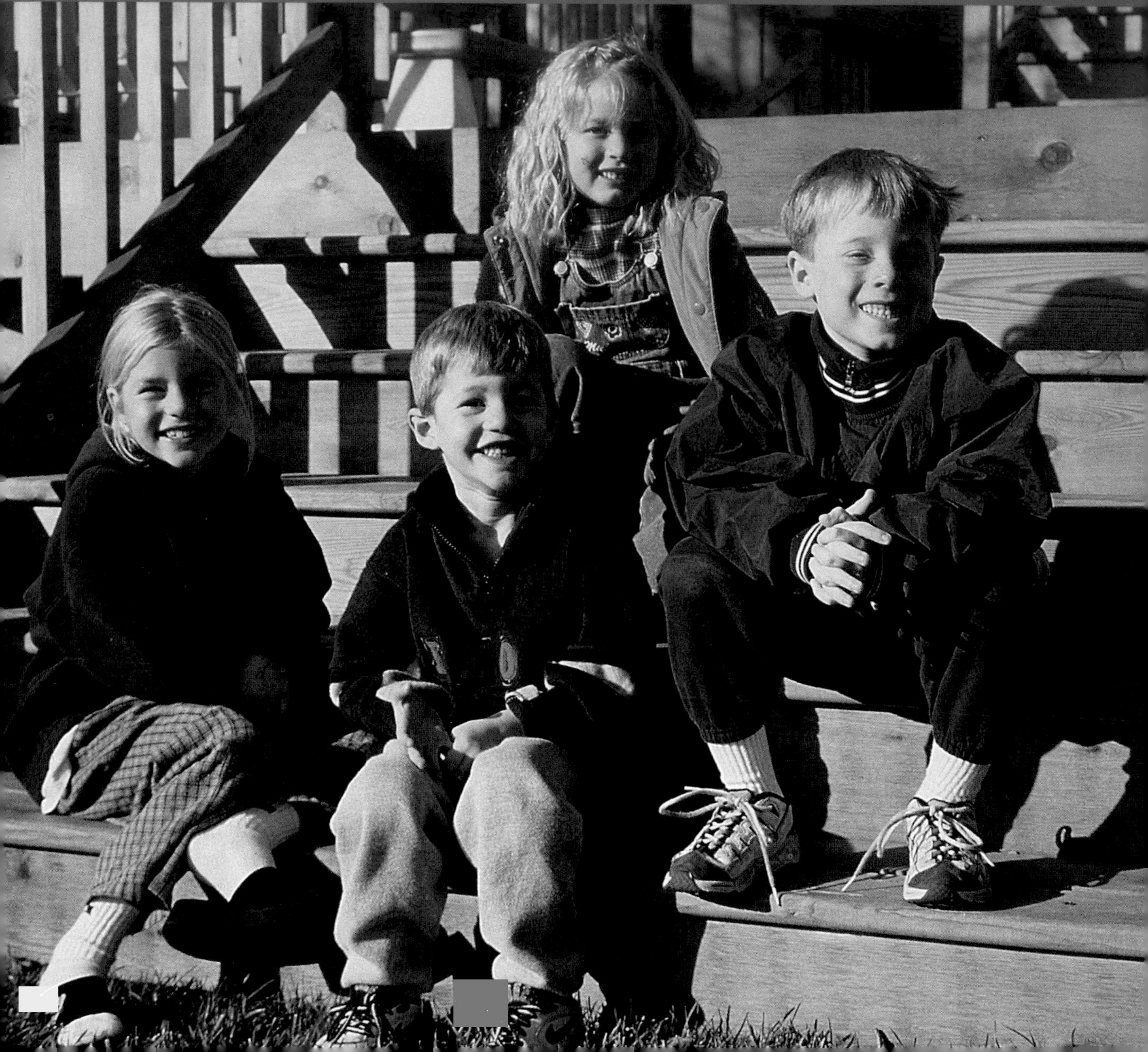

Cc

Cousins can look alike, or not!

Dd

Daddy cooks dinner on the grill.

Ee

Everyone gets a trophy.

Ff

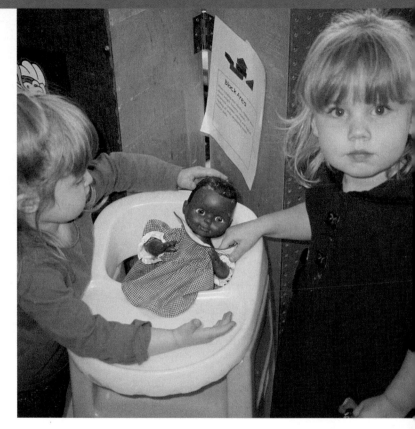

Friends share toys.

Gg

Great-grandpa tells stories.

Hh

Holidays bring families together.

17

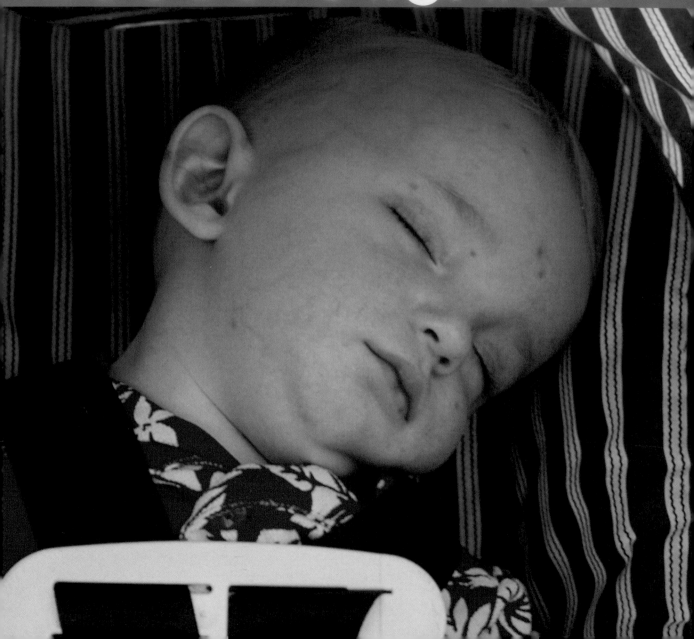

Infants need a lot of sleep.

Jj

"Junior" shares his dad's name.

A B C D E F G H I J K L M

Kk

Kith means friends.

Ll

Love feels good.

Mm

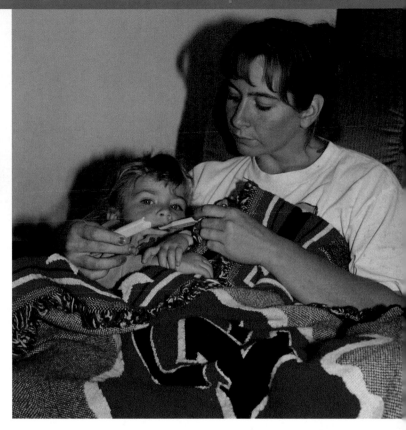

Mommy helps you feel better.

25

Nn

New neighbors may be shy.

Old people need hugs, too.

Pp

Parents play with their kids.

Qq

Quiet time is good for reading.

Rr

Reunions gather families.

Ss

Sisters and brothers are siblings.

Tt

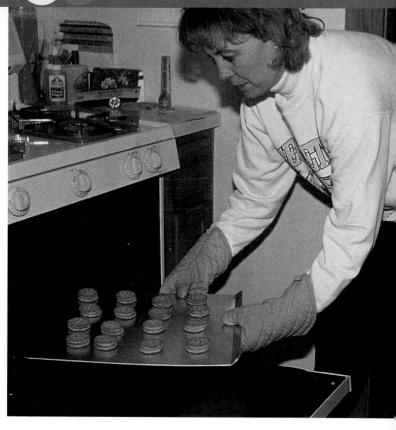

Treats come from mom's oven.

Uu

Uncles and aunts visit.

ABCDEFGHIJKLM

Vv

Valentines show you care.

Ww

Weddings join families.

ABCDEFGHIJKLM

Xx

Extended family is nana, too!

Yy

You should help friends.

NOPQRSTUVWXY

Zz

Zany fun happens with family.